34ᵀᴴ CITY OF BURGOS POETRY PRIZE

PIXEL FLESH

AGUSTÍN FERNÁNDEZ MALLO

TRANSLATED BY
ZACHARY ROCKWELL
LUDINGTON

CARDBOARD HOUSE PRESS
www.cardboardhousepress.org
cardboardhousepress@gmail.com

CARNE DE PIXEL / PIXEL FLESH
Copyright © 2020 Agustín Fernández Mallo
Translation © 2020 Zachary Rockwell Ludington
Designed by Mutandis

First Edition, 2020
Printed in the United States of America
ISBN 978-1-945720-20-8
Distributed by Small Press Distribution
www.spdbooks.org

CARNE DE PÍXEL

AGUSTÍN FERNÁNDEZ MALLO

XXXIV Premio de Poesía Ciudad de Burgos

El espacio es todo él un solo espacio y el pensamiento es todo él un solo pensamiento, pero mi mente divide sus espacios en espacios de espacios y su pensamiento en pensamientos de pensamientos.

ANDY WARHOL

Quién hará esta música sonar,
reflejo de la vanidad,
cuando nadie quiera oírnos más.

FALSOS MITOS SOBRE LA PIEL Y EL CABELLO
LA COSTA BRAVA

Píxel [Picture Element]:
mínimo elemento de imagen que contiene toda la información visual posible.

*Space is all one space and thought
 is all one thought, but my mind di-
vides its spaces into spaces into sp-
aces and thoughts into thoughts
into thoughts.*

Andy Warhol

*Who will make this music play,
reflection of vanity,
when no one wants to hear us anymore.*

False myths about skin and hair
La Costa Brava

*Pixel [Picture Element]:
Smallest element of an ima-
ge containing all possible
visual information.*

mi cara digitalizada en el parpadeo de la pantalla. A mitad de la calle un portal, 1 m^2 de acera, 2 m^3 de aire, escenario en el que el tiempo [emboscado en su abstracción sin masa ni peso] a fin de encarnarse saqueará el recuerdo. El tiempo a tu lado me mostró que no hay más razones para creer en la imposibilidad de la vida después de la muerte de las que hay para creerla igualmente imposible antes. Que la luz que a cada instante llega y te hace feliz y bien hecho son besos que lanzaste y en forma de verdad irrefutable [invisible] regresan [quién ve la luz]. Que la soledad del *sprinter* supera a la del corredor de fondo no porque llegue primero, sino porque imagina que llegará primero; pero, adónde. Sin habla, mirabas fijamente, apretabas mi mano, llorabas y llovía. Vi claro en ese instante [suma de instantes] por qué era tan bueno el verso tan malo que antes de morir recitó aquel Replicante, porque *en tus ojos vi cosas que jamás ni yo ni nadie había visto, y todas se perderán* [son simultáneas muerte y vida] *como tus lágrimas en la lluvia.* No hubo esta vez ningún pájaro blanco al vuelo para decirnos que algo muere en luz saturada para que otra cosa nazca en vacío [lo dijo Heinsenberg, lo dijo Heráclito, lo dijo Burgalat, lo dijeron tantos]. Sólo transparente opacidad. Ahora yo ya sólo aspiro a las enumeraciones.

my digitized face in the blinking of the screen. Halfway down the street a door, 1 m^2 of sidewalk, 2 m^3 of air, a scene where time [stealthy in its massless weightless abstraction] will plunder memory in order to embody itself. My time by your side showed me there were no more reasons to believe in the impossibility of life after death than there are to believe that it's equally impossible before. That the light that arrives at every instant and makes you happy and well-made is kisses that you cast out, and that in the form of an irrefutable truth [invisible] come back [who sees the light]. That the sprinter's loneliness is more than the distance runner's not because he gets there first, but because he imagines that he'll get there first; but, where. Without speaking, you looked straight ahead, you were squeezing my hand, you were crying and it was raining. I saw clearly at that instant [sum of instants] why that line that was so bad was really so good, the line that Replicant recited before dying, because *in your eyes I saw things that neither I nor anyone had ever seen and they'll all be lost* [life and death are simultaneous] *like your tears in the rain.* This time there wasn't any white bird in flight to tell us that something dies in saturated light so that something else can be born in the vacuum [Heinsenberg said it, Heraclitus said it, Burgalat said it, so many have said it]. Only transparent opacity. Now I only aspire to enumerations.

fuiste la llama de mi razón alucinada. No había espacio donde apoyar ya mis símbolos. Te amaré tanto, decías, y aprendimos la importancia del café del desayuno en tanto yo salía a robar para ti naranjas. Devoramos el mundo, esa bestia sordomuda, para hacernos menos sordos, menos mudos, siguiendo una ley por la cual buscando crear y destruir energía la encuentras en belleza transformada. Yo no sabía qué pasa cuando un péndulo se detiene porque jamás había visto uno detenido. Llorabas y llovía. Vi cosas en tus ojos que nadie había visto, me apretabas la mano buscando exprimir aquella fruta robada a mí; a nadie; transgénico zumo de lluvia en lágrimas. La verdad es a veces tan verdad que se vuelve 100% cristalina, y así innombrable.

you were the flame of my astounded reason. There wasn't any space anymore to set my symbols on. I'll love you so much, you were saying, and we learned the importance of coffee at breakfast, while I was heading out to steal oranges for you. We devoured the world, that deaf-mute beast, to make us less deaf, less mute, following a law by which searching to create and destroy energy you find it transformed into beauty. I didn't know what happens when a pendulum stops because I had never seen one stopped. You were crying and it was raining. I saw things in your eyes that no one had seen, you pressed my hand trying to squeeze the stolen fruit out of me; out of nobody; transgenic rain-juice in tears. The truth is sometimes so true that it becomes 100% crystalline, and thus unnamable.

lo más difícil de narrar siempre es el presente. Su instantaneidad no admite proyecciones, fantasías, desenfoques. Yo no sé si todo aquello existió porque no sé si existe. No sé si son ciertas tus manos [aunque sí sé que verosímiles] bajo la lluvia, y tus ojos como Polaroids [irrepetibles y mostrando más de lo previsto]. Llorabas. Llovía. Quién deja a quién si todos andamos diferidos de nosotros mismos, dejando atrás lo que entendemos para no entender lo insoportable: que cada cual es uno y además no numerable, que vendrán otras, que vendrán otros, que asusta pensar hasta qué punto todos somos intercambiables. Sé que no podré olvidar cuanto vi en tus ojos: el aire ionizado sobre nuestras cabezas, tus manos apretadas [no sé exactamente qué visión pretendían refutar]. Puede que fuera yo quien lloraba, puede que fuera en mí donde llovía. Puede que aún me estés besando, o que aquel martes [por decir un día] jamás haya existido.

the hardest thing to narrate is always the present. Its instantaneity doesn't allow for projections, fantasies, loss of focus. I don't know if all of that existed because I don't know if it exists. I don't know if your hands are true [though I do know they're believable] in the rain, and your eyes like Polaroids [unrepeatable and revealing more than expected]. You were crying. It was raining. Who's leaving whom if we're all going around delayed from ourselves, leaving behind what we understand, in order not to understand what we can't handle: that everyone is one and, what's more, not numerable, that other women will come, that other men will come, that it's scary to think about the extent to which we're all interchangeable. I know I won't be able to forget all I saw in your eyes: the ionized air above our heads, your clasped hands [I'm not sure exactly what vision they were trying to refute]. It could have been me who was crying, it could have been in me where it was raining. It could be you're still kissing me, or it could be that Tuesday [to pick a day] never existed.

asusta pensar que el mundo construido por los amantes sea tan microscópico como larvado e incomunicable, pero es lo único que nos salva de otro susto de iguales dimensiones que es la muerte. La acera se hizo más verde porque otra luz apareció entre nosotros. Circunvalamos la ciudad en silencio. Llovía. Me invitaste a un Lucky, a fuego. No recuerdo si nos besamos. Te quise tanto y tan de verdad, te dije. Después, cada cual subió sus propias escaleras hacia leyes de la noche que convergen en alambres, insomnios; a mi pesar, literatura. Lo que vi en tus ojos corre el peligro de olvidarse porque ni nadie lo había visto ni nadie lo verá ya, y por destruir el silencio repetí mentalmente la cita de aquel libro de Valente que un día te dejé en el buzón de voz; hablaba de la única evidencia impalpable [de qué si no]; la noche que me dijiste de dónde vienes cuando regresé del WC y al contestar ya dormías. Soñabas un futuro necesariamente mejor. Después, ya digo, cada cual hacía sus propias escaleras: objeto de impredecible y doble dirección: microscopía que elaboran los amantes. Replicantes de un código de barras que jamás llegamos a vivir.

it's scary to think that the world built by lovers could be just as microscopic as it is hidden and incommunicable, but it's the only thing that saves us from another scare just as big which is death. The sidewalk got greener because another light appeared between us. We circled the city in silence. It was raining. You offered me a Lucky, a light. I don't remember if we kissed. I loved you so much and so for real, I said. Afterwards, each went up their own stairs to laws of night that converge in wires, insomnia; despite myself, literature. What I saw in your eyes runs the risk of being forgotten because no one had seen it and no one will ever see it, and to destroy the silence I repeated in my mind the quote from that book by Valente that I left on your voicemail one day; it had to do with the only intangible evidence [if not, what else]; the night when you said to me where'd you come from when I came back from the bathroom and when I answered you were already sleeping. You dreamt a future better by necessity. Afterwards, like I said, each one to their own stairs: object of a double and unpredictable direction: microscopy that lovers perform. Replicants of a barcode that we never end up living.

*Las galaxias crecen
por procesos de fusión con otras
galaxias, dice Günter Hasinguer del
Instituto Max Planck, Alemania.*

*Las galaxias espirales,
que muestran mucha
formación estelar,
se unen y dan lugar a una elíptica.
Pero sus agujeros negros también
se acaban fusionando, y se convierten
en agujeros negros supermasivos
que expulsan el gas
de la recién formada galaxia elíptica.
Ése parece ser el panorama.*

Galaxies grow
through processes of fusion with other
galaxies, says Günter Hasinguer of the
Max Planck Institute, Germany.

Spiral galaxies,
    which exhibit abundant
    star formation,
join and become an elliptical galaxy.
But their black holes also
end up fusing and become
supermassive black holes
that expel the gases
of the recently formed elliptical galaxy.
This seems to be the panorama.

todo es superficie porque sólo existen trayectorias, porosas de sí, no vemos más que lo que hunden nuestros pies. Los alrededores: metáforas de esa soledad. Mirabas mi rostro durante horas en silencio cada noche. Todo es superficie. Hasta el amor carece de raíz: llorabas, llovía, esa agua sólo buscaba el riego que lo prendiera a la tierra, pero la tierra no existe, te digo. El agua se inventó para inocularnos la ficción de los campos de fuerzas, de la compañía, de un hilo de mensajes que vertical nos atraviesa. No así la luz, que se frena en la piel y pone en marcha el ansia del beso. Lo que vi en tus ojos jamás nadie lo vio, que fuimos la vida secreta del agua, y un juego de cuerpos para revalidar esa fuga sin cifra por la cual el ser humano es algo más que un trozo de saliva. Como todas las cosas que importan, nuestra alucinación no tuvo contemporáneos: un cristalizar sin agua, sin hilo argumental. Lo recuerdo. Hubo un día en que por primera vez vi pájaros desde tu ventana, creí que ellos también nos miraban, no lo entendí como el presagio de lo que vendría, sólo existen trayectorias y a ambos lados una luz que al fin se oxida entre dos manos apretadas en la despedida. Fuiste la llama de mi razón alucinada. El álgebra de mi transformación en animal: como ellos, a tu lado morí y no supe que había muerto [bendita seas], me volví inmortal. Divino tu cuerpo por catastrófico, radical, una línea de costa; por fractal.

everything is surface because only trajectories exist, themselves porous, we don't see any more than what sinks under our feet. Surroundings: metaphors for that loneliness. You would look at my face for hours in silence every night. Everything is surface. Even love lacks roots: you were crying, it was raining, the water was only searching for the kind of irrigation that would hold love down to earth, but earth doesn't exist, I'm telling you. Water was invented to inoculate in us the fiction of force fields, of company, of a string of messages that cuts across us vertical. Not so with light, which brakes on skin and kicks the wish for a kiss into gear. What I saw in your eyes no one ever saw before, that we were the secret life of water, and an interplay of bodies to revalidate that cipherless escape by which a human being is something more than a bit of saliva. Like everything that matters, our astonishment had no contemporaries: crystallization without water, without a plotline. I remember. There was a day when for the first time I saw birds from your window, I thought they were also watching us, I didn't understand it as the premonition of what would come, only trajectories exist and on both sides a light that in the end oxidizes between two hands squeezing each other in goodbye. You were the flame of my astounded reason. The algebra of my transformation into an animal: like them, at your side I died and I didn't know that I had died [bless you], I became immortal. Your body divine because it's catastrophic, radical, a coastline; because it's fractal.

[en algún lugar lo tengo escrito], las artes surgieron con el único propósito de anular el peso, y de entre todas la más sublime es la pareja. Tu portal, la calle, la cuesta. Hay en esta clase de despedidas una extraña antiley acuática [llorabas, llovía] que sumerge al Principio de Arquímedes y lo invalida. Nada hay más melancólico que una lengua de lava ladera abajo, ebria de destrucción y directa a la atrofia, sin embargo. Me sujetabas muy fuerte la mano, sin habla mirabas fijamente, la goma recogía tu pelo en otro territorio menos experimental, más conocido, mapa de cuerpos planos que copulan en la noche [qué hermética paradoja, qué miedo o soledad los maneja]. Ya no hay tu rostro porque no hay centro, no hay centro porque no hay fin, no hay fin porque *fin* es una palabra que ahora mismo no comprendo. Pesaba sobre tu cuerpo y el mío la terrible certeza de llegar siempre tarde a nosotros mismos: por eso nos los prestamos un día [y todo cuanto eso arrastra]. Después, las flores, los hoteles, las cartas, arquitectura de domingo extasiados en edificios feos de verano y costa, como decía aquella canción de Paraíso, hasta que circunvalamos la ciudad y me invitaste a un Lucky, a fuego, una noche de martes por primera vez sin objetivo, sin rumbo, *rumbo* era una palabra extraña, estorbaba, como el apéndice estorba al intestino, que lo atrofia, o la solución a la incógnita, que la deslía, hasta que llegamos a tu calle, llorabas, llovía, me cogiste fuerte mi mano, descubrimos sin palabras otra certeza: que ya nunca llegaríamos tarde el uno al otro, que cualquier próximo día podría esperar a ser el último y, sin embargo, había que elegir éste para decir adiós.

[I've got it written down somewhere], the arts developed with the sole purpose of nullifying weight, and among them all, the most sublime is the couple. Your door, the street, the hill. There is in this kind of goodbye a strange aquatic anti-law [you were crying, it was raining] that submerges Archimedes' Principle and invalidates it. There's nothing more melancholy than a tongue of lava down the mountainside, drunk on destruction and straight to atrophy, anyway. You held on to my hand really tight, you were looking straight ahead without speaking, a hair tie held your ponytail in another less experimental territory, better known, a map of flat bodies that copulate at night [what hermetic paradox, what fear or loneliness controls them]. Your face is no more because there's no center, there's no center because there's no end, there's no end because *end* is a word that I don't understand right now. Weighing over your body and mine was the terrible certainty of always arriving late to ourselves: that's why we lent them to each other one day [and everything that gets dragged into that]. Afterwards, the flowers, the hotels, the letters, Sunday architecture, ecstasy in ugly buildings of summer and seaside, like that Paraíso song said, until we circled the city and you offered me a Lucky, a light, a Tuesday night for the first time with no objective, no destination, *destination* was a weird word, it got in the way, like how the appendix blocks the intestine, it atrophies it, or the solution to the enigma, that unties it, until we got to your street, you were crying, it was raining, you grabbed my hand tight, we discovered without words another certainty: that from then on we would never arrive late to each other, that any coming day could expect to be the last and, nonetheless, we had to pick this one to say goodbye.

desconocías el Principio de Mínima Acción por el cual la luz [todo en general] busca el camino más rápido para viajar entre dos puntos. Circunvalamos la ciudad contradiciéndolo cuanto pudimos. Partíamos del fin; en realidad no nos movimos. Pasamos por delante de unas excavaciones [fibra óptica, cableado, comunicaciones Siglo21], e hice una broma acerca de aquella mujer y aquel hombre que encontraron abrazados en la excavación de Pompeya. La escena salía en *Viaje a Italia*: los descubrieron mientras filmaban. Ingrid Bergman también entonces se había echado a llorar. Partir de un recuerdo equivale a partir del fin, los recuerdos se construyen para el último día aunque nos engañe su gen de pasado. En realidad, no nos movimos. Me invitaste a un Lucky [frase entre tus dedos], y en esa cinética apariencia encontramos el exceso, la belleza para alcanzar lo que al llegar al fin nos convirtió en algo más que una frase para el fin, algo más que una ecografía de riñón, que un isótopo, un punto de luz que no desapareció porque nunca partió. El camino infinito de verdad más corto.

you didn't know the Principle of Least Action by which light [everything in general] seeks the quickest path to travel between two points. We circled the city contradicting it as much as we could. We started at the end; in reality we didn't move. We passed in front of a dig site [fiber-optics, cables, 21st Century communications], and I cracked a joke about the woman and the man they found holding each other in the excavation of Pompeii. The scene was in *Journey to Italy*: they found them while they were filming. Ingrid Bergman also had started crying then. Starting out from a memory equals starting from the end, memories are constructed for the last day even if their gene of past deceives us. In reality, we didn't move. You offered me a Lucky [a phrase between your fingers], and in that kinematic appearance we found excess, the beauty to reach what, getting to the end, made us into something more than a phrase for the end, something more than a sonogram of a kidney, than an isotope, than a point of light that didn't disappear because it never started out. Truly the shortest infinite path.

en aquel hotel de Capri te vi como realmente eras, sagrada, violenta, promiscua, dulce, ingenua, en resumen A.H., frente a Tiffany's desayunando resaca con diamantes. Pero diga lo que diga Oriente, el mal existe, se da en cierta forma de cohabitar contrarios. Nos hicimos una foto desnudos en el espejo, que por alguna ley física no salió. Exceso de perfección, capilaridad. Se anulan los símbolos, se descomponen los cuerpos, paradoja que invalida y funda el miedo. Estabas tan entera con aquellas botas de punta; tan propiamente distante en la Casa Malaparte. Hiciste muchas fotos al letrero *Circunvesubiana*, cinturón de ferrocarril que rodeaba al Vesubio, su rumor humeaba: bestia cansada que circunvalamos también en silencio aquel último martes en otra ciudad lejana sin centro ni criterio.

in that hotel in Capri I saw you as you really were: sacred, violent, promiscuous, sweet, naïve, in summary A.H. in front of Tiffany's, having a hangover with diamonds for breakfast. But whatever the East says, evil exists, it shows up in a certain way that opposites cohabitate. We took a picture naked in the mirror, that due to some physical law didn't come out. An excess of perfection, capillarity. Symbols are nullified, bodies decompose, a paradox that invalidates and establishes fear. You were so whole with those pointy boots; so truly distant in the Casa Malaparte. You took a lot of pictures of the *Circunvesubiana* sign, the train-belt that circled Vesuvius, its rumble let up smoke: tired beast that we also circled in silence that last Tuesday in another distant city without center or criterion.

Sin embargo, no se sabe aún

si las fusiones de galaxias y agujeros negros

son propias de una etapa concreta

de la evolución del universo.

Puede que fueran más abundantes

en el pasado, pero la propia Vía Láctea se unirá

a la de Andrómeda dentro de unos pocos

miles de años.

Y será un proceso desigual.

Nonetheless, it is still unknown
if the fusions of galaxies and black holes
are specific to a particular stage
of the universe's evolution.

It is possible that they were more frequent
in the past, but even the Milky Way will join
with Andromeda within some few
thousand years.
And it will be an uneven process.

llegó cada cual con su pasado [lo que equivale a decir futuro programado]. Sin que lo supieras, en cada hotel de Nápoles robaba papel higiénico, *una muestra*, digamos, para al regresar escanearlo y ver manar en la pantalla del PC el azar ordenado en un surtido de puntos negros sobre blanco, mapa de píxeles en los que leer una cifra, un vacío que, siendo profano en cierto modo es sagrado, píxeles garantes de aquel silencio que la alquimia buscaba en los objetos y yo busqué en ti [tus manos de joven modelo retirada, tu lengua muda en el beso]. Al escaneo surgieron mapas, figuras, cosas, reflejos de lo que vendría y que nunca te enseñé, dos Replicantes en busca de una vida más convencional, oxígeno de mortal que no los asfixiara. A este escaneado lo llamaré pixelado n° 1 [yo ya sólo aspiro [[lo advertí]] a las enumeraciones].

each of us came with their past [which is the same as saying programmed future]. Without you knowing, in every hotel in Naples I would steal toilet paper, *a sample,* let's say, to scan upon returning home, to watch the ordered chance of an assortment of black points over white flow onto the PC screen, a map of pixels in which to read a cipher, an emptiness that, being profane, is in a certain way sacred, pixels guaranteeing that silence alchemy had sought in objects and that I looked for in you [your young retired-model hands, your tongue mute in a kiss]. The scan revealed maps, figures, things, reflections of what would come and what I never showed you, two Replicants in search of a more conventional life, mortals' oxygen that wouldn't suffocate them. I'll call this scan pixelation n$^{\circ}$ 1 [now I only aspire [[I said it before]] to enumerations].

circunvalamos la ciudad en silencio, aunque era mayo llovía. O frío. Es difícil entender qué valor se adensa en un beso cuando es todos los besos y al mismo tiempo la única cifra, qué peso específico comprime pero revalida cierta fe [por decir algo] en tu *línea de universo* cuando un hombre y una mujer toman la decisión de circunvalar una ciudad en silencio. Hay algo en el silencio que llama al frío; no así al calor, que agita sin romper la barrera del sonido y amplifica las palabras, sobre todo cuando se unen los cuerpos de quienes se aman. Después te quedabas muda todas las noches durante horas mirándome. Qué clase de muerto o frío era yo ya entonces, te digo. Quiero pensar que no veías en mí este final de zapatos helados, de barcos detenidos que vimos al llegar a la línea de costa, de bobinas interminables de fibra óptica ciega aún o durmiendo. Pero tampoco veías ese Big Bang que [lo dicen los cosmólogos] era espuma cuántica, caos de masas solitarias cegadas por la utopía de un futuro Universo perfecto [después se desvió para dar lugar a la Tierra, al cero cósmico, al hombre y su residuo de amor]. Quiero pensar que era tu piel tan suave que yo no la sentía. Sólo eso.

we circled the city in silence, even though it was May it was raining. Or cold. It's hard to understand what value is condensed in a kiss when it's every kiss and at the same time the only cipher, what specific weight compresses but revalidates a certain faith [to say something] in your *world line* when a man and a woman make the decision to circle a city in silence. There's something in silence that calls up the cold; but not heat, which shakes the sound barrier but doesn't break it, which amplifies words, especially when the bodies of people who love each other come together. Afterwards you would sit in silence every night looking at me for hours. What kind of dead or cold was I by then, I'm telling you. I want to think that you didn't see in me this ending of frozen shoes, of standing ships that we saw when we got to the coastline, of endless spools of fiber-optic cable still blind or sleeping. But you couldn't see that Big Bang either, which [cosmologists say it] was quantum foam, a chaos of lonely masses blinded by the utopia of a perfect future Universe [afterwards it detoured to give way to Earth, to cosmic zero, to man and his remainder of love]. I want to think that your skin was so smooth that I didn't feel it. Only that.

al llegar a casa pusiste el CD de Organ y, vestida aún de fiesta, al salir del baño dejaste la sortija de brillantes y las lentillas sobre la mesa desierta [de la cocina también desierta]. Símbolos que no puedo explicar. Me sobrepasan. Podría llamarlos pixelado n° 2, pero aquella noche devino puramente analógica, y la más bella analogía fue la contraída entre aquellos dos objetos que abandonaste y los dos horizontes de tu cuerpo: el vivo y el muerto. Así hasta el amanecer trabajó tu sexo.

when we got home you put on the Organ CD and, still dressed to go out, coming out of the bathroom you left your diamond ring and your contacts on the empty table [in the kitchen, also empty]. Symbols I can't explain. They go beyond me. I could call them pixelation nº 2, but that night became purely analogical, and the most beautiful analogy was the one made between two objects that you left behind and the two horizons of your body: the living and the dead. And so your sex worked until the morning.

huyen los pájaros de las cosas curvas, de las circunvalaciones, de los programas bien configurados. Está en las virtudes del pájaro solitario. Una heladería en el centro de Sorrento, me escribiste una frase dudosa con mi diccionario de italiano para turistas. No hay ornamento ni retórica donde manda la luz, por artificio que ésta parezca. Robé la cucharilla, un diseño antiguo nunca visto, te dije. La agitación de tu pelo en el Spider descapotable, me dije. Escribiste muchas postales con un punta de 0.5 mm y letra casi de imprenta, *ornamento retórico de 2ª especie* se le llama a eso en Teoría del Diseño. Bostezaba entretanto. Me llevé el papel higiénico y al escaneo surgió una línea moteada en negro, sucesión de acontecimientos idénticos, la página llena de puntos suspensivos que Bretón tituló *El Paseante* o, [lo llamaré pixelado n° 3], tu respiración al correr tras esa forma de desaparición a la que llamamos Mundo.

birds flee from curved things, from circular routes, from well-configured programs. It's among the virtues of the solitary bird. An ice-cream shop in the center of Sorrento, you wrote me a questionable sentence with my Italian dictionary for tourists. There is no ornament or rhetoric where light rules, as much as light might seem an artifice. I stole the little spoon, an old design, never before seen, I told you. The movement of your hair in the Spider convertible, I told myself. You wrote lots of postcards with a 0.5 mm pen and handwriting almost like a printing press, *2nd variety rhetorical ornament* it's called in Design Theory. Meanwhile I yawned. I took the toilet paper and a black dotted line came out in the scan, a succession of identical events, the page full of ellipses that Breton titled *The Flâneur* or, [I'll call it pixelation n° 3], your breathing when chasing after that form of disappearance that we call World.

Hasta hace 5 años,

los agujeros negros eran

poco más que una construcción

teórica,

una hipótesis para observaciones que

no se explicaban de otra manera.

Pero ahora,

por primera vez,

vemos cómo el espacio-tiempo

se curva y rota

en torno a un agujero negro.

Until 5 years ago,
black holes were
little more than a theoretical
                    construct,
a hypothesis for observations that
could not be explained any other way.
                    But now,
                    for the first time,
we can see how space-time
bends and spins
around a black hole.

la primera vez que estuvimos a solas eras una mujer detenida, pero no en el espacio, no en el tiempo, sino en otra cosa más compleja [que no complicada], en una de esas imágenes atravesadas por haces ¿de lejía? ¿de miedo?, por mujeres que has amado, por todas las ciudades que has circunvalado, por la música que se nos roba en la infancia y no vuelve, salvo como vuelve en ruido lo perdido, por el primer beso que se recuerda, por el último que olvidas, por la materia prima de la soledad, metafísica del todo absurda, por las flores que con el tiempo te llevaría al trabajo y despuntarían al calor del PC, [quién lo diría, sudor de circuitería], por la definición de cuerpo a secas: conglomerado de conductos o flores según se carezca o no de amor, por el sexo que en una habitación de Italia aún nos faltaba por romper [pasada la frontera, el cabello pierde la memoria], por el mapa en tus manos de joven modelo retirada el primer día, tu abandono en el sofá, tu lengua de agua. Así detenida te fuiste haciendo agua que corrió. Yo no sé si fue lo mismo que vi en tus ojos cuando al final llorabas y llovía.

the first time we were alone together you were a woman standing still, not in space, not in time, but in something more complex [though not complicated], in one of those images crossed by streaks, of bleach? of fear?, by women that you've loved, by all the cities you've circled, by the music stolen from us in childhood that doesn't come back, except the way what's lost comes back in noise, by the first kiss you can remember, by the last one that you forget, by the raw material of loneliness, a totally absurd metaphysics, by the flowers that with time I'd bring to you at work and that would unfurl with the heat from your PC, [who would have thought, circuit-board sweat], by the bare definition of body: conglomeration of conduits or flowers depending on whether love is lacking, by the sex in a room in Italy that we still hadn't broken [hair loses its memory across the border], by the map on your hands, hands of a young model, retired from day one, your idle relaxation on the couch, your tongue of water. Standing still like that you started becoming water that flowed. I don't know if it was the same thing I saw in your eyes when in the end you were crying and it was raining.

circunvalamos la ciudad. Aunque ya era mayo, hacía frío y llovía. *Que el mundo es un lugar horrible*, escribió Sabato en *El Túnel*, *es una verdad que no necesita demostración.* Entonces, me digo, por qué persistimos en demostrarlo. Lo llamaré pixelado n° 4.

we circled the city. Even though it was already May, it was cold and it was raining. *That the world is a horrible place*, Sabato wrote in *The Tunnel*, *is a truth that does not require demonstration.* Then, I say to myself, why do we insist on demonstrating it. I'll call it pixelation n° 4.

por mucho que se circunvale, la ciudad inventa límites, y llegamos al mar. Espeso, carnoso: al borde de cualquier forma. Mareo que precipita al observador [estábamos tan enteros, tan sólidos, tan para un final], mar en tu sexo que era víscera y flor en el beso. Y, sin embargo, vi uno de esos mares ascéticos, paisaje digital, sin referencias, ecografía de riñón, de hígado, antesala del feto y de la vida que imaginamos, pero no tuvimos. Fuiste toda la carne que unas manos pueden llegar a abarcar [y, sin embargo, un segundo, un rayo indefinido, un salto cuántico].

no matter how much you circle it, the city invents limits, and we end up at the sea. Thick, fleshy: on the verge of any form. Waves of nausea that hurl the observer forward [we were so whole, so solid, so ready for an ending], sea in your sex that was viscera and flower in the kiss. And, still, I saw one of those ascetic seas, a digital landscape, without a referent, a sonogram of a kidney, of a liver, the prelude of a fetus and of the life we imagined, but didn't have. You were all the flesh that hands can span [and, nonetheless, a second, an indefinite ray, a quantum leap].

a las personas les ocurre a veces lo que a la memoria, mutan en personajes descarnados, meros vectores de ideas. Te voy a cuidar tanto, decías. Drogarse, leer novelas, follar: hábitos de mediocres, te decía. Hay algo más fuerte que la carne, el impulso suicida del aliento cuando toma aire; el impulso homicida cuando se espira. Jadeabas; no sé a cuál te referías. Lo alucinante en la anfetamina no es tomarla sino observar el arco de medio punto que describe su curvatura [es condición de lo bien hecho atravesar los siglos sin rozamiento], pero esto no basta con decirlo, hay que entenderlo. A veces cuesta toda una vida, lo llamaré pixelado n° 5.

the same thing that happens to memory sometimes happens to people, they mutate into fleshless characters, just vectors of ideas. I'm going to take such good care of you, you said. Doing drugs, reading novels, fucking: the habits of mediocre people, I told you. There is something stronger than flesh, the suicidal impulse of breath when it takes in air; the homicidal impulse of exhaling. You were panting; I don't know which one you were referring to. The mind-blowing thing about amphetamines isn't taking them but observing the semicircular arc traced by their curvature [it's a characteristic of well-made things to cross centuries without friction], but it's not enough to say it, you've got to understand it. Sometimes it takes a whole lifetime, I'll call it pixelation n° 5.

circunvalar una ciudad empapada, meditando aquel martes sin meditar nada; cara boquiabierta; pide masa. Buscan quienes se aman un final patético, la apariencia de un mal en el que consolarse, Ingrid Bergman llorando ante una mujer y un hombre que la muerte hace siglos sorprendió abrazados. Estéril muerte entre la lava; lo que hoy los hace útiles, precisos. Estabas tan bella, tan entera con tus botas de punta en aquel viaje, la mujer más exacta y occidental que jamás había visto, luz dominada entre tus manos, frases: tiralíneas en tus labios, alucinado equilibrio al especiar el pescado. Tan entera con tus botas de punta en aquel viaje, cuando aún eras sólida [pero no lava], cuando, como en las canciones de Low, era tu fuerza una antigravedad, una extravagancia inoperante, un CD mil veces regrabado.

circling a soaking city, meditating on that Tuesday without meditating on anything; a jaw-dropped face; begging for mass. Those who love each other are looking for an ending with pathos, the appearance of an evil in which to console themselves, Ingrid Bergman crying in front of a woman and a man that death surprised centuries ago in an embrace. Sterile death in lava; what makes them useful today, necessary. You were so beautiful, so whole with your pointy boots on that trip, the most thorough and western woman I had ever seen, light dominated by your hands, sentences: a drafting pen between your lips, astounded balance as you seasoned the fish. So whole with your pointy boots on that trip, when you were still solid [but not lava], when, like in Low's songs, your strength was an antigravity, a useless extravagance, a CD reburned a thousand times.

Son los primeros instrumentos
capaces de detectar el tipo
de radiación que emite la materia
cuando cae hacia un agujero negro.
Es una materia muy caliente, y emite
básicamente
su "último grito" en forma de rayos X.

They are the first instruments
capable of detecting the type
of radiation that matter emits
when it falls towards a black hole.
It is very hot matter, and it emits
essentially
its "last cry" in the form of X rays.

fortalecida en iones el agua de tus ojos, en nubes bajas. La Casa Malaparte, colmillo de otro horizonte, habita sólo en sus propias fotografías. También el glamour que envuelve a tus botas de punta vive dentro de tus botas de punta; y no hablo de los pies; hablo del veneno. He leído que el veneno es el veneno, pero el veneno adulterado qué es. Lo llamaré pixelado n° 6.

the water in your eyes fortified with ions, with low clouds. Casa Malaparte, the canine tooth of another horizon, it resides only in its own photographs. Also the glamour surrounding your pointy boots lives inside your pointy boots; and I'm not talking about your feet; I'm talking about poison. I've read that poison is poison, but adulterated poison, what is it. I'll call it pixelation n° 6.

tú y yo nunca llegamos a discutir de estética, lo único que nos unía. Lo único porque estética y ética son lo mismo, una pose ante el mundo. Discutimos y mucho de esas otras visiones en apariencia simples, como abrazarte por detrás para besarte y ver pájaros desde tu ventana. Quisimos interpretarlos, interrogar la honestidad de la naturaleza, sin saber que tal cosa no existe, que todo es artificio. Hasta que mi mano telarañándose más abajo de tu cintura. Cerrabas los ojos [bendita seas]. Yo con tu Lucky hacía un agujero en un mapa.

you and I never argued over aesthetics, the only thing that united us. The only thing because aesthetics and ethics are the same thing, a pose before the world. We argued plenty about those other visions, simple in appearance, like hugging you from behind to kiss you and seeing birds from your window. We tried to interpret them, to interrogate the honesty of nature, without knowing that such a thing doesn't exist, that everything is artifice. Until my hand spiderwebbing its way past your waistline. You closed your eyes [bless you]. With your Lucky I was making a hole in a map.

yo he ganado y perdido muchas horas mirando el ascenso vertical de las burbujas del agua con gas en un vaso. Una velocidad constante que, según cierto principio de relatividad, equivale a decir nula. Un ascender para hundirse en la atmósfera [que según San Juan de la Cruz equivale a decir tierra]. La mano sin óxido en la que me sumerjo. Y me la das sabiendo que no hay futuro en el fondo de los vasos, salvo para organismos simples, unicelulares, fango que queda tras la caída de un cosmos, el hueco que deja su propia trayectoria. No hay célula más simple que el beso aunque su fuerza invalide las distancias y el espacio [o la luz [que es el espacio]], aunque todo aquello se corrompa ahora en este ascenso de burbujas vertical y nulo, en esta sombra de la luz que es decir más luz, esta semblanza del silencio, este moteado cuántico en la pantalla del cual *no se puede hablar y hay que callar* como dijo el maestro en el Punto 7 y al que llamaré [es natural] pixelado n° 7.

I've gained and lost many hours looking at the vertical ascent of bubbles in sparkling water in a glass. A constant velocity that, according to a certain principle of relativity, is the same as saying null. An ascent just to sink into the atmosphere [which for San Juan de la Cruz is the same as saying earth]. The unoxidized hand into which I submerge myself. And you give it to me knowing that there is no future at the bottom of a glass, except for simple organisms, unicellular, slime that's left after the fall of a cosmos, the emptiness left by its own trajectory. There is no cell simpler than the kiss even if its strength invalidates distances and space [or light [which is space]], even if all of that gets corrupted now in the ascent of these bubbles, vertical and null, in this shadow of light which is to say more light, this semblance of silence, these quantum dots on the screen, *whereof one cannot speak, and thereof one must be silent* like the master said in Proposition 7 and which I'll call [it's only natural] pixelation n° 7.

No es que los actuales telescopios
de rayos X vean los agujeros negros en sí.
Ni siquiera la luz puede
escapar a la fuerza gravitatoria
de estos objetos que, por tanto, son invisibles.

Lo que se observa con rayos X es
la materia que
está siendo atraída hacia los agujeros negros,
hasta una distancia muy próxima al llamado
"horizonte de sucesos" (el punto
de no retorno de la materia que cae)

It is not that contemporary X-ray
telescopes can see black holes themselves.
Not even light can
escape the gravitational force
of these objects that, thus, are invisible.

What can be observed with X rays is
the matter that
is being pulled towards black holes,
up until a distance very close to the so-called
"event horizon" (the point
of no return for falling matter)

sé que tú y yo nunca llegamos hasta el fondo, que no tocamos el fango del verdadero contacto, esa intransferible complicidad producto del espejismo llamado pareja. Nuestro espejismo se quedó en superficie, espejo, flores que nadie decapita: mueren confiadas en un paisaje que ya no las necesita y, como tú en mí y yo en ti, se descubren al poco tiempo por otras intercambiables. Lo que hay. Asusta pensarlo. Lo dijo Bataille [aunque de otra manera]: hay en toda cultura una *parte maldita*, un excedente intercambiable, condenado a ser dilapidado hasta el manar de su esencia, y esto es lo que precisamente nos hace irracionales, humanos, lo que fuimos, eternos objetos de supermercado [ahora recuerdo aquella estación de servicio].

I know that you and I never got to the bottom, we never touched the slime of true contact, that intransferable complicity that's a product of the mirage called a couple. Our mirage remained a surface, a mirror, flowers that no one decapitates: they die believing in a landscape that doesn't need them anymore and, like you in me and me in you, it soon turns out they're other, interchangeable ones. Just the way it is. It's scary to think it. Bataille said it [though in a different way]: there is in every culture a *cursed part*, an interchangeable surplus, condemned to be broken down to the flowing of its essence, and this is precisely what makes us irrational, human, what we once were, eternal supermarket objects [now I remember that gas station].

[no es descabellado], se podría suponer que lo que no llegamos a vivir resultó del todo prescindible. Nadar en verano, cambiar de coche, comentar un poema de Burroughs, proyectar un hijo, pasar juntos un constipado. Pero yo me adhiero a lo que decía Brines, *no desdeñes los placeres vulgares, tienes la edad justa para saber que se corresponden exactamente con la vida,* [o algo así].

[it's not crazy], you could suppose that what we didn't get to live turned out to be totally unnecessary. Swimming in summer, switching cars, talking about a Burroughs poem, planning for a kid, getting over a cold together. But I stick to what Brines said, *don't spurn simple pleasures, you are just the right age to know that they correspond exactly to life*, [or something like that].

hay una fotografía que no se borra. A mi derecha una niña muy mona con diadema. A mi izquierda un niño con camisa de cuadros hasta la nuez. Yo ante una tarta que soplar [cuento 8 velas], boquiabierto, demasiado exacto como para inducir una semblanza, circunvalando una espera, una finitud, mi esguince de luz.

there's a photograph that doesn't fade. To my right a cute little girl with a tiara. To my left a boy with a checkered shirt buttoned all the way up. Me in front of a cake to blow out [I count 8 candles], mouth open, too exact to invoke a resemblance, circling an expectancy, a finiteness, the spraining of my light.

recordar un hecho real dentro de un sueño equivale a dotarlo aún de más realidad: dos límites lo acotan: anochece y amanece. El abrazo mientras dormías para llevar tú mi mano hacia tu pecho con tibia [no sé cómo expresarlo] ensoñación no soporta tal exceso de realidad y en mitad de la noche me despierto.

remembering a real event in a dream amounts to conceding it even more reality: two limits define it: it dusks and it dawns. The embrace while you were asleep bringing my hand to your chest with warm [I don't know how to express it] dreaminess can't survive such an excess of reality and in the middle of the night I wake up.

También se sabe hoy
que los agujeros negros iluminan
el universo en mayor proporción
de lo estimado.

Today we also know
that black holes illuminate
the universe to a greater degree
than had been estimated.

hay algo en el píxel de carnal y abstracto, cuadriculada superficie que contiene toda la información visual posible, agota su sentido, y sin embargo es una cifra, está vacío. Hay en el píxel una metafísica. Origen, piel acristalada, proteico paisaje, *el viajero que llegando a Región*. Más tarde cada cual fue concibiendo su sembrado de rosas cúbicas, cubículo, cubicaje [como quieras llamarlo]. Ganó tu sexo en nitidez. Fracasó en particular la carne de las rectas para llegar a lo único que son, $y=ax+b$; letras. El resto, arrebato de lo que no existe: ficción: pura espectroscopia.

there's something fleshy and abstract in the pixel, a squared surface that contains all possible visual information, its meaning is exhausting, nonetheless, it's a cipher, it's empty. There's a metaphysics in the pixel. Origin, glazed skin, a protean landscape, *the traveler who, arriving in Región.* Later each of us went about imagining their crop of cubical roses, cubiculary, cubicity [whatever you want to call it]. Your sex increased in clarity. In particular the flesh of straight lines failed, becoming only what they are, $y=ax+b$; letters. The rest, the rapture of what doesn't exist: fiction: pure spectroscopy.

que el tiempo pasa y nos vamos descomponiendo, es algo que está muy claro. Que no sabemos qué es eso que se nos descompone, también. Que el hecho de ir hacia una muerte inmortal después de la muerte nos convierte ahora en zombis, en vivientes muertos, clarísimo. Pero que el beso sea una célula elaborada necesariamente en silencio, es un hecho que, lo admito, no comprendo.

the fact that time passes and we decompose is something that's very clear. That we don't know what it is that decomposes in us, ditto. That the fact of moving towards an immortal death after death now turns us into zombies, into living dead: super clear. But that a kiss is a cell developed necessarily in silence is a fact that, I admit it, I don't understand.

(a) He encontrado una nueva forma de felicidad que está también en el equilibrio del funambulista [en el propio equilibrio], en el instante en que suspende la visión el parpadeo, en el pájaro que aletea para permanecer quieto, o en el punto en que se cruzan dos cartas con mensajes probablemente contrarios [pero hay que continuar, te dije, hay que continuar], en el punto en el que la levedad iguala al peso: cuando no siento ni hastío ni hambre y es como si desapareciese el cuerpo. **(b)** A veces llegué a pensar que en algún futuro [las fotos son recién nacidos que no crecen] seríamos como Leonard Cohen y Susan en esa foto que tanto mirábamos de Leonard Cohen y Susan: incorruptibles, unicelulares, glamour químicamente puro, envidiados, elegantes: un nuevo estado [$6°$] de la materia. **(a∩b)** No sé cuál de los dos estados es metáfora del otro, si la metáfora se inventó para dar vida a todo lo mal muerto y una vez resucitado aniquilarlo para siempre. En esa emboscada se resume todo este ADN postpoético.

(a) I've found a new form of happiness that's also in the tightrope walker's balancing act [in balance itself], in the instant in which a blink suspends vision, in the bird that beats its wings to stay still, or in the point in which two letters with probably opposite messages cross paths [but we've got to keep on, I told you, we've got to keep on], in the point in which lightness equals weight: when I don't feel boredom or hunger and it's as if my body disappeared. **(b)** sometimes I came to think that in some future [photos are newborns that don't grow] we'd be like Leonard Cohen and Susan in that photo of Leonard Cohen and Susan that we used to look at all the time: incorruptible, single-celled, chemically pure glamour, envied, elegant: a new state [6th] of matter. **(a∩b)** I don't know which of the two states is a metaphor for the other, since metaphor was invented to give life to everything not-quite-dead and, once revived, to annihilate it forever. In that camouflage is the summary for all this postpoetic DNA.

pone en marcha el amor una genética imparable, una fuerza que lo derriba todo, incluso teorías sólidamente comprobadas [no hay enemigo más fácil de vencer que el perfectamente dibujado]. Es por eso por lo que los naturalmente esclavos buscamos amos muy visibles, omnipotentes: vulnerables. Rodear aquel martes la ciudad era entrar en un nuevo estado [6º] de la materia. Después uno subió y otro bajó [elige tú] una misma escalera: hacia los amaneceres de finales de noche que te configuran en cero para crear el vacío; hacia los amaneceres de principio de día que le estrechan la cintura al cero para despertarte infinito.

love kicks an unstoppable genetics into gear, a force that knocks over everything, even solidly-tested theories [there's no easier enemy to defeat than the one that's perfectly delineated]. That's why we natural slaves seek very visible masters, omnipotent masters: vulnerable ones. Going around the city on that Tuesday we entered a new state [the 6th] of matter. Afterwards one of us went up and the other went down [you pick] the same flight of stairs: towards the dawns of the ends of nights that configure you in zero in order to create a vacuum; towards the dawns of the beginnings of days that squeeze in zero's waist to wake you up infinity.

*Los telescopios espaciales de rayos X
han demostrado, por ejemplo,
que todas las galaxias tienen un
agujero negro en su centro.*

*Deep-space X-ray telescopes
have demonstrated, for example,
that all galaxies have a
black hole at their center.*

siendo sincero, no sé qué significa la palabra *lluvia*, ni la palabra *ojos*, ni *perder* ni *ver*, y aún menos frases como *vi cosas en tus ojos que ni yo ni nadie había visto, y todas se perderán como tus lágrimas en la lluvia*. Sólo sé que entre tus brazos fui una estrella mundial [bendita seas], y que tu arruga en este mapa es el equilibrio de un pájaro solitario que se derrumba [como siempre la belleza] en el cenit de su vuelo [bendita seas][2]. Me mirabas cada noche muchas horas en silencio, células de sonido revuelto, *siento escalofríos cuando veo tu cuerpo joven y que tu alma ya no está en su lugar,* nos cantaba Antonio Vega [bendita seas][n] en una radio que le compramos a un chino, hasta que el eco mutó en ceniza y alguien en las ondas dijo basta.

to be honest, I don't know what the word *rain* means, or the word *eyes*, or *lose* or *see*, and even less sentences like *I saw things in your eyes that neither I nor anyone had ever seen and they'll all be lost like your tears in the rain.* I only know that in your arms I was a global star [bless you], and that your wrinkle in this map is the balance of a solitary bird that tumbles down [as always with beauty] at the zenith of its flight [bless you][2]. You would look at me every night for hours in silence, cells of scrambled sound, *I get chills when I see your young body and that your soul isn't in its place anymore*, Antonio Vega would sing to us [bless you][n] on the radio that we bought from a Chinese guy, until the echo mutated into ashes and someone on the waves said that's it.

comprobar que eras más bella [hallazgo inesperado] desnuda que vestida, y tu ropa interior un *horizonte de sucesos*, lugar cuyo radical significado conocen muy bien los cosmólogos [ahora no me extenderé; sólo diré que ya no somos víctimas de lo que brilla incomprensible en la esquina del cronómetro, en la velocidad de la luz].

confirming that you were more beautiful [unexpected discovery] naked than dressed, and that your underwear was an *event horizon*, a place whose radical significance is well-known to cosmologists [now I won't get carried away; I'll just say that we're no longer victims of that incomprehensible glow in the corner of the stopwatch, in the speed of light].

para mí siempre fue un misterio el origen de tu ropa interior, de su perfecta cabida en tu cuerpo. Inversa es la lógica de quien descubre una tierra analógica pero real como la de un espejo. Pero si te fijas, la imagen del espejo no responde exactamente a la real, el espejo posee una pátina, que aunque invisible, la oscurece, como si algo de materia se perdiese en el trayecto, un residuo que si lo juntaras, verías lo que pierde aquel que te mira; mejor dicho, quien en tu imagen desaparece; o, aún mejor, quien en ti ya ha desaparecido.

for me the origin of your underwear was always a mystery, its perfect fit to your body. Inverse is the logic of one who discovers a world that's analogical but real, like the world in a mirror. But if you look close, the image in the mirror doesn't correspond exactly to the real one, the mirror has a patina that, though invisible, darkens the image, as if some of the matter were lost in the span, a remainder that, if you gathered it up, would let you see what the person looking at you is missing; to put it better, who disappears in your image; or, even better, who in you has already disappeared.

la radio, una canción de The Smiths que ya entonces era vieja, *take me out tonight because I want to see people and I want to see lights*, en el descapotable hacia donde el Sol foguea el horizonte [bien podría ser un cartón-piedra de Las Vegas, la Ciénaga de Manganelli, o tierra bajo tierra]. Como en *Encadenados*, me abrazas. Perdida en un bosque de resacas más ficticias que reales, me encontraste en un claro. Te detuviste a recordar cómo era la luz, su porqué, quién la creó [dijiste que yo]. Ya tus ojos eran brújulas orientadas verticalmente hacia arriba; pero el cielo no tiene horizonte, pensé, salvo ese gélido eco que nos llega del Big Bang llamado *radiación de fondo*. La memoria no está en la maquinaria, sino en la grasa de los relojes, [te pones el sostén derecho]. Pero el tiempo no es el mal, sino una crónica obsesión padecida por las cosas que no las deja definirse. Ambos sabíamos que la longitud de una carretera en algún mapa [sólo hay que buscarlo] equivale a la combustión de un cigarro, que las películas son mentira, y el horizonte el cable tenso contra el que, ignorante, aceleras. Me besas, me abrazas, ingenua tarareas con la radio, *to die by your side, such a heavenly way to die.*

the radio, a song by The Smiths that was already old then, *take me out tonight because I want to see people and I want to see lights*, in the convertible towards where the Sun cooks the horizon [it could easily be a paper mâché Las Vegas, Manganelli's Swamp, or an underground world]. Just like in *Notorious*, you hug me. You were lost in a forest of hangovers, more fictional than real, and you found me in a clearing. You paused to remember what light was like, its reason, who created it [you said I did]. Your eyes by then were already compasses oriented vertically, pointing up; but the sky doesn't have a horizon, I thought, just that frigid echo that reaches us from the Big Bang called *background radiation.* Memory isn't in machinery, but in the grease in clocks [you put on the right side of your bra]. But time isn't evil, just a chronic obsession things have that won't let them define themselves. We both knew that the length of a highway on a map [you just have to look for it] equals the combustion of a cigarette, that movies aren't real, and that the horizon is the tensed cable against which, unaware, you accelerate. You kiss me, you hug me, naïvely you hum along to the radio, *to die by your side, such a heavenly way to die.*

De todas formas,

el que a cada galaxia le corresponda

un agujero negro ya se venía

                    sospechando.

At any rate,
the fact that every galaxy has its
own black hole had for a while been
suspected.

es cierto, había mucha noche, lluvia, una mujer, etc, pero en realidad únicamente hablo de mí, porque es lo único que tengo. No tengo distancia. Sólo esta proximidad tan nula que por fortuna invalida cualquier juicio moral. Odiábamos la moral. Circunvalamos la ciudad. Ionizado y oscuro el cielo, me invitaste a un Lucky [estrella entre tus dedos]. *En un radio de 2000 km alrededor de la Tierra hay más de 2 millones de quilos de chatarra*, decía el periódico: satélites, cohetes, artefactos desintegrados en su circunvalar. Fríos. Silenciosos. Amorales [otra moral]. La realidad es sus símbolos [y no hay más], y, sin embargo, no podemos estar simultáneamente a ambos lados del radio de la Tierra.

it's true, there was a lot of night, rain, a woman, etc., but in reality I'm only talking about myself, because that's all I have. I don't have distance. Just this proximity that's so insignificant that luckily it invalidates any kind of moral judgment. We hated morality. We circled the city. The sky ionized and dark, you offered me a Lucky [star between your fingers]. *Within a radius of 2000 km around Earth there are more than 2 million kilos of scrap*, the newspaper said: satellites, rockets, devices disintegrated in their circling. Cold. Silent. Amoral [another morality]. Reality is its symbols [and there's nothing more], and, still, we can't simultaneously be at both ends of Earth's radius.

sin fatiga, caminas, circunvalas la ciudad; adormecidos los detalles. Existe un punto en el que la tangente corta a la circunferencia; siempre está ahí, o quiere desaparecer [que es lo mismo]. Lo dijo Canetti, *no merece la pena desear venganza, se cumplirá, se cumple automáticamente por un principio de reversibilidad que hay en las cosas.* Entiéndelo.

without getting tired, you walk, you circle the city; the details are sleepy. There's a point where the tangent cuts through the circumference; it's always there, or it's trying to disappear [which is the same thing]. Canetti said it, *wishing for revenge isn't worth it, it'll happen, it happens automatically because of a principle of reversibility that's in everything.* Understand that.

nada posee una finalidad, nada agota su fuego, porque no hay dirección donde no hay gravedad. Porque adentro todo es nada. Y adentro es afuera. Y afuera no existe. Hasta el texto se escribe a sí mismo [compón tú ahora el símil con el camino que trazas, con esa circuitería entre metafísica y física que fue tu cuerpo en mi abrazo]. Cuanto existe debió haber resonado antes en el silencio, hasta el beso se empapa en la esponja de ese eco [cristalino, asexuado] que sin materia se propaga. Parte la palabra del silencio para, extrañamente, buscar el silencio. Lo encuentra cuando muere, cuando se fibrosan palabras como *lluvia*, *azul,* o *pájaro* en la Lluvia, en el Azul, o en el Pájaro.

nothing possesses a finality, nothing uses up its fire, because where there's no gravity, there are no directions. Because on the inside everything is nothing. And inside is outside. And outside doesn't exist. Even a text writes itself [now compose the simile with the path you trace, with that circuitry somewhere between metaphysical and physical that was your body in my arms]. All that exists must have resonated before in the silence, even a kiss gets soaked by the sponge of that echo [crystalline, unsexed] that propagates itself without matter. The word sets out from silence, strangely, to search for silence. It finds it when it dies, when words like *rain*, *blue* or *bird* fiberize in the Rain, in Blue or in the Bird.

[no sólo en vertical] hay otra forma de ver las cosas. En ocasiones la lluvia en toda su extensión es una gasa que no cae, únicamente cubre, cuando ya no alfilerea, cuando lo que duele es tan amplio que no se alcanza a ver su curvatura, cuando ese instante es una de esas urbanizaciones reticuladas, cenicientas, crecidas en un desierto de Arizona al servicio de una carretera por la que ya nadie pasa. Pero ahora tú. Yo digo que llorabas y llovía porque lo vi en tus ojos. Pero no lo vi. Yo digo que circunvalamos la ciudad porque me pareció su curvatura inabarcable, porque se busca lo que no se tiene para destruirlo, porque al llegar al puerto vimos barcos en los que imaginé que nos íbamos, porque el aire pesaba ionizado en contrarios, porque nunca los cables de fibra óptica fueron más fibra y menos óptica, porque nunca una zanja fue más netamente zanja, más víscera, menos matemática. Pero, sobre todo, porque nunca fueron materia más equivalente la lluvia y la lava [también Ingrid Bergman se había echado a llorar cuando los encontraron].

[not just vertically] there's another way of seeing things. Sometimes rain in all its extension is a gauze that doesn't fall, it just covers, at least when it doesn't poke holes, when what hurts is so wide that you can't see its curvature, when that instant is one of those gridded housing developments, ashy, sprouted from the Arizona desert in the service of a highway that no one drives by on anymore. But now you. I say you were crying and it was raining because I saw it in your eyes. But I didn't see it. I say we circled the city because its curvature seemed limitless to me, because a person looks for what they don't have in order to destroy it, because when we got to the port we saw boats I imagined us leaving in, because the air was heavy, ionized in opposites, because fiber-optic cables never were more fiber and less optic, because a ditch never was so completely ditch, more visceral, less mathematical. But, more than anything, because rain and lava never were more equivalent matter [Ingrid Bergman also started crying when they found them].

pasa un camión, compongo
un haiku:

cae un hombre
por la ventana, lógi-
camente muere

a truck goes by, I compose
a haiku:

man falls
out window, logi-
cally, he dies

detenida y sola, no existe agua que corra, porque su paisaje siempre fue más agua. También tú te prolongas hasta donde tu mirada alcanza; nada se opone. Lo veo porque ya estoy afuera. Es hermoso contemplar cómo hasta el silencio se desentiende del silencio y hay que empezar a escribir palabras en vacío, 1 portal, 1 m^2 de acera, 2 m^3 de aire, narcótica matemática, sin axioma, transformar tu buhardilla en otras coordenadas [por ejemplo, Los Ángeles], poner un CD de Dominique A, imprimir una foto en la que salgan flores que crecen al calor de un PC. No pasaron tan rápido el otoño y el invierno, más bien aún giran el uno en torno al otro, ciegos, sin que nada se les oponga. [Esto me recuerda a otra cosa, pero no sé a qué.]

standing still and alone, no flowing water exists, because its landscape always was more water. You also extend yourself as far as your eyes can reach; nothing in opposition. I see it because I'm already outside. It's beautiful to contemplate how even silence acts like it can't hear silence and you've got to start writing words in the empty space, 1 door, 1 m^2 of sidewalk, 2 m^3 of air, mathematical narcotics, with no axioms, turning your loft into other coordinates [for example, Los Angeles], putting on a Dominique A CD, printing a photo of flowers growing in the heat of a PC. Fall and winter didn't go by that fast, it's more like they're still spinning around each other, blind, with nothing opposing them. [This reminds me of something else, but I don't know what.]

circunvalamos la ciudad en silencio, me invitaste a un Lucky [escala real entre tus dedos], resulta fácil medir lo imposible, sólo hay que permanecer en silencio, esencia del instrumento más antiguo del mundo, que viene a ser el sueño nocturno. Pero cómo medir lo posible, te digo, experta en el arte más antiguo del mundo, aquel que dentro del perímetro de los platos de porcelana se consume a medida que se representa, enmudecer ante ese lenguaje hecho de alimentos resucitados, donde lo abstracto se organiza en el perímetro de los platos [y todos los sentidos barajabas en el centro]. Tú nunca hiciste comida muerta.

we circled the city in silence, you offered me a Lucky [actual size between your fingers], turns out it's easy to measure the impossible, you've just got to be silent, the essence of the oldest instrument in the world, which turns out to be a dream at night. But how to measure what's possible, I'm telling you, expert in the oldest art in the world, the art that within the perimeters of porcelain plates consumes itself in its own performance, going mute before that language made of resuscitated meals, where abstraction organizes itself inside the perimeter of the plates [and you ran through all the meanings in the center]. You never made dead food.

una demostración de que la Tierra no es redonda es que cavando un hueco nunca llegas al otro lado; ardes antes en el centro. Tampoco todo esto posee una antípoda; se extingue el hilo de la tinta antes de alcanzar su contrario. Pero hilo cuanto más profundo, más frío: yendo hacia el incendio de tu cuerpo, no hace más que regresar al mío. A la gangrena. Al tejido congelado que da argumento a estas horas reflectantes.

one proof that the Earth is not round is that by digging a hole you never get to the other side; you burn up before in the center. All this doesn't have an antipode either; the thread of ink runs out before reaching its counterpart. But a thread that, where deeper, is colder: going towards the incineration of your body, it just turns back to mine. To gangrene. To the frozen tissue that gives a plot to these reflectant hours.

nos gustaba ver películas juntos, y llorar de risa en los finales cursis, nunca en los amargos, fingir que sabíamos lo suficiente de estética y vida como para distinguir lo bueno de lo malo. Al final no fue así, tú llorabas y llovía, y era francamente malo y amargo. Aprender a gestionar la fantasía de un solo golpe.

we liked to watch movies together, and cry from laughing at the cheesy endings, never at the bitter ones, pretending that we knew enough about aesthetics and life to distinguish good from bad. In the end that's not how it was, you were crying and it was raining, and it was frankly bad and bitter. Learning to act out fantasy all at once.

Pero el resultado

más impactante que se constata es

el papel clave de los agujeros negros

en la construcción del universo.

El escenario global

que se dibuja es que las primeras

estrellas que se formaron,

cuando el universo era muy joven,

eran muy masivas, y por eso

murieron muy rápidamente.

But the most

stunning revelation of this research is

the key role that black holes played

in the creation of the universe.

The general pattern

that comes to light is that the first

stars to form,

when the universe was very young,

were very massive, and so

they died very quickly.

el misterio más profundo está en la materia. Compraste unas postales, sencillas, vulgares, escribiste lo que se escribe en tal espacio programado, en torno a nosotros unas mujeres venían con la compra, turistas manoseaban chatarra, llegaba el barco Nápoles-Capri cargado de cuerpos sin sexo, te saqué una foto [botas de punta, gafas, Saimaza Mezcla], te miraba. El camarero arrancó la cuenta de la caja registradora, aún debes de tenerla, verdadero poema, [lo llamaré pixelado n° 0]: el misterio más profundo está en la materia.

the deepest mystery is in matter. You bought some postcards, simple ones, tacky, you wrote what one writes in such a programmed space, around us some women were returning home with groceries, tourists looking through the trash on offer, the Naples-Capri boat was arriving full of sexless bodies, I took a photo of you [pointy boots, sunglasses, Saimaza coffee], I was staring at you. The waiter tore the bill out of the cash register, you probably still have it, a true poem, [I'll call it pixelation n° 0]: the deepest mystery is in matter.

metálicos en un jardín botánico, extraños a ese paquete de luz desleída por ambos [no venía del horizonte], cada vez más lejos de esa única tangente que es al fin arena en un colchón o epidermis vacía, así, venía diciendo, *metálicos en un jardín botánico*, circunvalamos una elipse de 2 centros. Sólo eso. 2 centros.

metallic in a botanical garden, foreign to that package of light we both let fade [it didn't come from the horizon], continually further from that only tangent which is, in the end, sand on a mattress or empty skin, so, as I was saying, *metallic in a botanical garden*, we circled an ellipse with 2 centers. Only that. 2 centers.

scan of toilet paper, Hotel Bristol bathroom, Capri

escaner de papel higiénico, WC Hostal Bristol, Capri

AFM, 2002

Créditos y agradecimientos

Las partes en verso son diferentes extractos del artículo *Agujeros negros, constructores del cosmos*, originalmente en prosa, editado por el diario *El País*, el 2 de noviembre del 2005, firmado por Mónica Salomé.

De las citas que encabezan el texto, la de Andy Warhol pertenece a su libro, *Mi filosofía de A a B y de B a A*, (Tusquets Editores), y la cita de la Costa Brava pertenece a su LP, *Llamadas perdidas* (Mushroom Pillow, 2004).

El resto de citas insertadas en el texto (poemas, novelas, o canciones), son más o menos de memoria. Siento los errores que pudiera haber cometido. Supongo que, como decía el gran Michi Panero, *lo que importa al final es la idea*.

Quiero agradecer al jurado del XXXIV Premio de Poesía Ciudad de Burgos haber visto en este libro motivos suficientes para hacerlo merecedor del premio. También a DVD Ediciones por acogerlo, y a cuantos han apoyado desde el principio mis propuestas, por descabelladas que fueran.

Por lo demás, la presencia de un barco varado en una estepa al dar una curva sigue siendo la peor de las pesadillas.

CREDITS AND THANKS

The verse sections of this book are various extracts from the article "Black Holes, Builders of the Cosmos," originally in prose and in Spanish, published by the daily newspaper *El País* on 2 November 2005 under Mónica Salomé's byline.

For the quotes at the outset of the text; Andy Warhol's is from his book *The Philosophy of Andy Warhol (From A to B and Back Again)* and the quote from Costa Brava comes from their LP, *Llamadas perdidas* (Mushroom Pillow, 2004).

The rest of the quotes inserted in the text (poems, novels, or songs) are more or less from memory. I'm sorry for any mistakes I might have made. I guess, like the great Michi Panero used to say, *what matters in the end is the idea.*

I'd like to thank the jury of the 34th City of Burgos Poetry Prize for having seen in this book sufficient motive to deem it worthy of the prize. Also, thanks go to DVD Ediciones for giving it a home, and to everyone who has supported my projects from the beginning, however crazy they were.

As far as the rest goes, coming out of a curve to find a ship grounded on the steppes is still the worst of all nightmares.

Dedicatoria

A la cocina del 1° A del n° 4 de la calle Estudio General, Palma de Mallorca, lugar en el que escribí este libro.

DEDICATION

To the kitchen of apartment A, first floor at nº 4 calle Estudio General, Palma de Mallorca, the place where I wrote this book.

THIS TRANSLATION IS DEDICATED TO GUSTAVO PELLÓN.

Agustín Fernández Mallo takes his book titles from pop-culture icons like classical Hollywood actresses (*Joan Fontaine Odisea (mi deconstrucción)*, 2005) or Spain's favorite hazelnut-flavored chocolate spread (*Nocilla Dream*, 2006, followed by the other titles in the *Nocilla* trilogy). He uses compositional techniques that befuddle any reader looking for a straightforward book of poems in the case of the former or a clear-cut narrative in the case of the latter. In the present translation I render into English a book in which Fernández Mallo remains true to his incongruous form, juxtaposing *Blade Runner* with Wittgenstein; spectroscopy with Juan Benet's unsettling novel *Volverás a Región*; The Smiths with the science of black holes, and repeating, withholding, and mixing information, references, and registers.

With a wryness seen before in *Joan Fontaine Odisea*, which Fernández Mallo dedicates to the memory of the defunct Spanish national electrical company in gratitude for the warmth of his childhood nights, *Carne de píxel* (I call it *Pixel Flesh*) is dedicated to the kitchen in the apartment where the poems were composed. Along with this dedication goes the author's apology for errors or misquotes throughout the text, as he works from memory. In the interest of the unsettled and palimpsestic feeling this gives the original, my translation maintains misspelled names (for example, the correct spelling of the Max Planck scientist's name: Günther Hasinger; the correct spelling for the train at Mount Vesuvius: la Circumvesuviana). I've also followed Fernández Mallo in the slightly misapprehended quotes included in the text, such as Sabato's or the adapted quote from Roy, the Replicant in Ridley Scott's film.

I have refrained from inserting footnotes to comment on things like *The Flâneur*, a concept and a style certainly associated with Breton, to whom Fernández Mallo attributes authorship, but a text (*Le Flâneur des deux rives*) that really belongs to Guillaume Apollinaire. These intriguing little mysteries, pulled threads in the shared fabric of culture, are part of the interest of the book, and so explaining what Philip K. Dick or a perpetual motion machine might have to do with the characters' postcards would spoil part of the fun of *Pixel Flesh*. I have also attempted to produce something like the unusual syntax that Fernández Mallo exploits at times in the original, a favorite technique of his that can make meaning ambiguous and blur temporal or causal relationships. It also confers a weird dead-pan quality on many moments which press winkingly at the edges of sentimentality. These moments are copied, shuffled, and repeated throughout the book, producing a kind of feedback loop or hall of holograms reflecting and continually reconstituting the two characters, the reader, and pop images.

In the end, it is repetition that most profoundly marks this collection of poems [poems? Polaroids? samples?]. The repeated scenes and pop references constitute and define the speaker and his partner, but this repetition also means each image or attitude is a copy of something prior, at the same time eager to transfer its anxieties to its next incarnation [psychologists call it projection]. Thus, I felt I needed certain lexical correspondences to hold up in every instance – some words in the Spanish shouldn't have >1 rendering in my English. So, "soledad" is always "loneliness" and never "solitude"; "circunvalar" is always "circle" and never the plausible but awkward "circumambulate" or anything similar. Various tempting English choices for "cifra" ultimately don't work because they don't echo one another while offering nuance in individual instances nearly as well as "cifra" does in the Spanish. Thus, "cipher," with its many acceptable English definitions, fits all the uses well enough; it ought to allow a varied interpretation of the word in different places while still knocking repetitively on the same spot in the reader's mind [that aspiration of the brain].

In any translation, this is the best one can do, since no word can find its center in another language. There's recombination in the meiosis. I can't replicate a Replicant even if I see it twice, even if the original [but where is the original, I'm telling you] is the same as my reproduction. If it's raining or if you're crying I won't feel it the same as you [who]. Language can't take its measure in the rain if the rain takes shape in waves as well as particles [and a theory is a working model]. I'll manage in the thick of provisionality. And all that I manage to enumerate, all that I can convince you of, can't be compiled to a single sum, like the surface of your hair; because one thousand, 1,000, 1.000, *mil*, and back again across that many light years or *años luz* teases an asymptote [I said it before, these are working models]. *F*'s not quite *ma*, after all. There's bound to be a photon lost, a raindrop missed, a tear erased or stalled. The black hole's weight is guaranteed even if it only has itself for a center, and that's not a new idea. So in this translation, I wonder where the swallowed light or the raindrops go [all vectors depend, also, on perspective], what each red or blue shift portends, why each time you cry I relearn what is a tear? For lack of time [space] I'll call this pixelation n° n.

ABOUT THE TRANSLATOR

Zachary Rockwell Ludington is currently Assistant Professor of Spanish at the University of Maine. His research focuses on the poetry of Spain's historical avant-garde. He earned master's and doctoral degrees from the University of Virginia and a bachelor's from the University of North Carolina at Chapel Hill. His poetry and translations have appeared in *LEVELER, Bateau, PEN America, Drunken Boat,* and elsewhere. The present translation of Fernández Mallo's *Pixel Flesh* won a grant from the PEN/Heim Translation Fund in 2014.

ABOUT THE AUTHOR

Agustín Fernández Mallo was born in La Coruña, Spain in 1967. He is a specialist in hospital radiophysics, and he has been working in this profession over the course of twenty years. In 2000, he formulated the term and theory, *poesía postpoética* (postpoetic poetry), which investigates the connections between art and science. This is a topic he has explored in his poetry collections, *Creta Lateral Travelling* (2004, Cafè Món Prize), *Pixel Flesh* (2008, Burgos City Poetry Prize), and *Antibiótico* (2012), among others. His essay, *Postpoesía, hacia un nuevo paradigma*, was shortlisted for the Anagrama Essay Prize in 2009, and his recent novel, *Trilogía de la guerra*, won the Biblioteca Breve Prize. He is the author of six novels, including his acclaimed *Nocilla Trilogy*, published in translation by Thomas Bunstead, by Fitzcarraldo Editions and FSG.

CONTENTS

CPSIA information can be obtained
at www.ICGtesting.com
Printed in the USA
FSHW011141300720

9 781945 720208